VEGAN DIET (
FOR KIDNEY DISEASE

80+ Easy, Delicious Meatless And Plant-Based Recipes to Improve Your Renal Health And Nourish The Body

Nancy K. Doctor

Copyright © 2024 by Nancy K. Doctor

All rights reserved.
No part of this book may be reproduced in any form or by any electronic or mechanical means, including information storage and retrieval systems, without permission in writing from the publisher, except by a reviewer who may quote brief passages in a review.

FOR MORE COOKBOOKS ON RENAL DIET WRITTEN BY THE AUTHOR

Scan The QR Code Below

TABLE OF CONTENTS

"Food is medicine. Let your kitchen be your pharmacy, and your meals be your remedy.
The power to transform your health lies in your hands, and it starts with the choices you make in your kitchen."

- Nancy K. Doctor

INTRODUCTION

In the bustling world we live in, where time flies faster than a shooting star, it's easy to forget the importance of taking care of ourselves. But what if I told you that taking care of yourself could be an adventure in itself? What if I told you that you could embark on a journey to better health, all while indulging in delicious and nutritious meals that are not only good for your body but also your soul?

Welcome to "Vegan Diet Cookbook For Kidney Disease"! In this book, we're going to take you on a culinary journey like no other. But before we dive into the tantalizing recipes that await you, let me share a story with you; a story of hope, resilience, and the power of good food.

Nancy is just like any other 30-year-old, full of energy, curiosity, and a love for life. But there's one thing that sets Nancy apart, she's battling kidney disease. Every day, Nancy faces challenges that most young adults her age can't even imagine. From strict dietary restrictions to endless doctor appointments, her life is far from easy. But despite it all, Nancy remains determined to live life to the fullest.

One day, while flipping through the pages of a cookbook, Nancy Stumbled upon a recipe for vegan chili. Intrigued by the colorful ingredients and mouth-watering description, she decided to give it a try. As she chopped vegetables and stirred the simmering pot, something magical happened – she felt a sense of joy and purpose wash over her. For the first time in a long time, Nancy felt in control of her health.

With each delicious spoonful of chili, Nancy could feel her body thanking her. Gone were the days of bland, uninspired meals, she had discovered the beauty of plant-based cooking, and she was never looking back. From creamy hummus to savory frittatas, Nancy explored a world of flavors she never knew existed.

But Nancy's journey didn't end there. As she continued to experiment in the kitchen, she noticed something remarkable happening, her health was improving. Her energy levels soared, her kidney function stabilized, and her zest for life returned tenfold. And it was all thanks to the power of plants.

Inspired by her transformation, Nancy wanted to share his newfound love for vegan cooking with the world. Consequently, the comprehensive culinary guide titled "Vegan Diet Cookbook For Kidney Disease" came into existence. Packed with over 85+ mouth-watering recipes, helpful tips, and inspiring stories, this book is more than just a collection of recipes – it's a testament to the incredible healing power of food.

KIDNEY-FRIENDLY VEGAN RECIPES

The consumption and quantity of food and beverages can significantly impact your well-being when living with kidney disease. Our vegan recipes can help you feel your best while maintaining a kidney-friendly diet. Here are some delicious recipes that support Renal Diet and Vegan lifestyle;

Vegan Bean Bourguignon

Meal Type: Inspired Vegan Stew

Ingredients:

- One container (425 grams) of unsalted, canned black beans, thoroughly drained.
- ½ cup chopped fresh mushrooms
- 4 Medium onions, Spanish, diced
- ¼ Cup Cannellini Beans drained
- 3 cups Vegetable stock, no salt added
- 1 Carrot, medium diced
- 20g Parsley, roughly chopped
- 1 Tbsp Garlic, fresh, minced
- ½ tsp Black pepper
- 1 Tbsp Olive oil
- 1 tsp Smoked paprika
- 4 Tbsp Flour, all-purpose

- 3 sprigs Thyme, fresh
- Optional: Utilize ⅓ cup of red wine or water for deglazing

Directions:

1. Add oil to the pot or Dutch oven and sauté mushrooms with smoked paprika. Discard the mushrooms along with any excess fluids and reserve them for later use.
2. Add onions to the pan and cook until lightly browned. Incorporate the carrots and garlic, gently sautéing them.
3. Add the pepper, thyme, and flour.
4. Deglaze the pan with the wine, if using, or use water in its place.
5. Add vegetable stock, turn to medium-high, and stir until thickened. Reduce heat. Ensure to agitate the base thoroughly while mixing to dislodge any fragments adhering to the pot's bottom.
6. Add the beans. Allow the carrots to gently cook in the simmering liquid until they become tender, a process that should take around 20 to 30 minutes. Keep the pot uncovered on a simmer.
7. Add the mushrooms and any reserved liquid when 5 minutes are remaining.
8. Garnish with parsley.
9. Enjoy!

Roasted Red Pepper & Chickpea Hummus

Meal Type: Dips & spreads | Serving size: ⅕

Ingredients:

- ½ cup canned chickpeas, rinsed and drained
- 2 cups red pepper, cut into 2-inch wedges
- 2 garlic cloves
- 2 tablespoons extra-virgin olive oil
- 2 tablespoons lemon juice
- 1 tablespoon of tahini
- Black pepper to taste
- Optional: cumin, paprika, or chili pepper

Directions:

1. Preparation: Preheat oven to 400℉.
2. Lay out red peppers on a baking tray, and drizzle with a tablespoon of olive oil. Cook for 25 minutes, or until it reaches the desired softness.
3. Cool roasted peppers and add them to a food processor with chickpeas, garlic, tahini, lemon juice, extra virgin olive oil, salt, pepper, and other desired seasonings.
4. Blend until smooth.
5. Adjust consistency by adding water if too thick.
6. Transfer hummus to a serving bowl, and garnish with paprika if desired.

Vegan Tofu and Veggie Frittata

Meal Type: Breakfasts & brunch, Casseroles, Family Friendly | Prep Time: 30 minutes | Cooking Time: 60 minutes

Ingredients:

- 1 package (350 g) firm tofu, drained
- ¾ cup aquafaba (from cooked/canned chickpea)
- ¼ cup + 2 tbsp chickpea flour or all-purpose flour
- 1 medium potato, diced (1 cup)
- 1 medium red bell pepper, diced (1 cup)
- 1 large zucchini, diced (2 cups)
- 4 green onions, sliced (1 cup)
- ¼ cup cilantro, finely chopped
- 2 tbsp nutritional yeast
- 1.5 tbsp miso
- 1 tbsp garlic powder
- 1 tbsp onion powder
- ¼ tsp turmeric
- ¼ tsp sea salt
- 1 tsp red pepper flakes (adjust as needed)

Directions:

1. Preheat the oven to 350 °F.
2. In a blender, combine tofu, aquafaba, flour, nutritional yeast, miso, garlic powder, onion powder, turmeric, sea salt, and red pepper flakes into a smooth batter.

3. Dice red bell pepper, potato, and zucchini into small pieces. Finely chop green onions and cilantro.
4. Sauté diced bell pepper and potatoes in a pan for about 10 minutes until the potatoes are cooked.
5. Add zucchini, green onions, and cilantro. Cook the vegetables over medium heat until they reach a soft consistency, approximately 5 minutes.
6. Transfer the cooked vegetables into an 8-inch pie dish. Transfer the mixture to the vegetables, ensuring thorough integration.
7. Bake for 60 minutes until the top browns. Take the dish out of the oven and allow it to stand for several minutes to cool down. Slice and serve. Enjoy!

Vegan Instant Hearty and Bean Chili

Meal Type: Vegan Stew

Ingredients:

- 1 teaspoon Olive Oil
- 2 Small Green Peppers, chopped
- 1 Medium Onion, chopped
- 2 Cloves Garlic, chopped
- ¼ teaspoon Kosher Salt

- 1½ tablespoons Chile Powder
- 1 tablespoon Cumin
- ½ teaspoon Paprika
- 3 tablespoons Jarred Jalapeno Slices with Marinade
- 1-15 ounce (443 ml) can Low-Sodium Diced Tomatoes
- 1 cup Low-Sodium Chicken Stock
- 3 cups Water
- 1 cup of Bob's Red Mill 13-Bean Soup Mix, or 1 cup of a different variety of dried legumes
- Fresh Cilantro Leaves
- Fresh Jalapeno, sliced

Directions:

1. In the Instant Pot, add salt, chile powder, cumin, and paprika. Cook for 1-2 minutes until the spices become fragrant.
2. Add tomatoes, chicken stock, water, jalapeno slices with juice, and dried beans. Stir well.
3. Close and seal the Instant Pot, then set to pressure cook for 60 minutes. Once finished, allow it to naturally release for 10 minutes, and then manually release the pressure.
4. Serve in individual bowls and top with jalapeno and cilantro if desired.
5. For a non-vegan version, add 1 pound (453 g) of boneless, skinless chicken breast at

step 2. When the pressure has been released, remove the chicken breasts, shred them with a fork, and return the meat to the pot.

Light and Cheesy Summer Zucchini Lasagna

Meal Type: Main dish | Serving Size: ½ Cup |

Ingredients:

- 4 small zucchinis, thinly sliced
- ¾ of a cup (approximately 6 ounces) of finely grated plant-based mozzarella substitute (opt for a variety with under 250 milligrams of sodium per portion and free from phosphate or potassium enhancers)
- 2 tablespoons (2 oz) vegan parmesan cheese, grated (omit or replace for a vegan option)
- 2 tablespoons olive oil
- 1 clove garlic, minced
- 3 sprigs fresh thyme
- Pepper to taste

Directions:

1. Preheat your oven to 350°F.
2. Wash and trim the zucchini, then cut into slices using a mandolin. Season with pepper and set aside.

3. In a frying pan, heat olive oil. Add minced garlic and zucchini slices, sautéing for 4 minutes or until slightly softened.
4. In a greased medium-sized baking pan, add one layer of zucchini slices. Top with a layer of shredded vegan cheese.
5. Continue alternating layers of ingredients, finishing with a top layer of zucchini slices woven into a criss-cross formation. Top with grated vegan parmesan cheese and fresh thyme.
6. Cook for 15 minutes on the center rack, then broil on high until the topping is golden brown.

Hearty Vegetable Stew

Meal Type: Main Course

Ingredients:

- ½ onion, finely diced
- 2 stalks celery, finely diced
- 1 carrot, finely diced
- 1 bell pepper, finely diced
- 1 tablespoon garlic powder
- 2 teaspoons dried oregano
- 1 tablespoon chili powder
- 425 g kidney beans, rinsed and drained
- 425 g garbanzo beans, rinsed and drained
- 425 g black beans, rinsed and drained

- 1 tablespoon olive oil
- 14 ounces low-sodium vegetable broth

Directions:

1. In your slow cooker pot, combine all the ingredients.
2. Cook for 4 hours on high heat or 8 hours on low heat.

Plant-Powered Bean Stew

Meal Type: Wholesome Vegan Stew

Ingredients:

- One container (425 grams) of unsalted, canned black beans, with the liquid removed
- ½ cup chopped fresh mushrooms
- 4 Medium onions, Spanish, diced
- ¼ Cup Cannellini Beans drained
- Red wine (⅓ cup; optional), or use water for deglazing
- 3 cups Vegetable stock, no salt added
- 1 Carrots, medium diced
- 20g Parsley, roughly chopped
- 1 Tbsp Garlic, fresh, minced
- ½ tsp Black pepper
- 1 Tbsp Olive oil
- 1 tsp Smoked paprika
- 4 Tbsp Flour, all-purpose
- 3 sprigs Thyme, fresh

Directions:

1. Add oil to the pot or Dutch oven and sauté mushrooms with smoked paprika. Extract the mushrooms along with any excess juices and place them on one side.
2. Add onions to the pan and cook until lightly browned. Incorporate the carrots and garlic, lightly sautéing them in the pan.
3. Add the pepper, thyme, and flour.
4. Deglaze the pan with the wine, if using, or use water in its place.
5. Add vegetable stock, turn to medium-high, and stir until thickened. Reduce heat. Ensure thorough stirring by gently dislodging any bits adhering to the pot's base.
6. Add the beans. Simmer until the carrots are cooked. Approximately 20-30 minutes. Keep the pot uncovered on a simmer.
7. Add the mushrooms and any reserved liquid when 5 minutes are remaining.
8. Garnish with Parsley.
9. Enjoy!

Chef's Tips:

Add plenty of aromatics, such as Thyme and Rosemary, to boost the flavors of this classical French stew.

Hearty Shiitake Elixir

Meal Type: Soups & Stews | Serving size: ⅔ cup

Ingredients:

- 8 Cups Unsalted Vegetable or Chicken Stock
- 4 Whole Green Onions
- 4 oz. Fresh or Dried Shiitake Mushrooms
- 2 Tbsp Ginger (keep in sizable pieces)
- 2 Whole Garlic Cloves

Directions:

1. Add all ingredients to the pot. Heat until boiling, then lower the temperature to maintain a gentle simmer.
2. Simmer for 40 minutes to 60 minutes.
3. Strain and reserve liquid.

Harmonious Carrot and Apple Fusion

Meal Type: Soups & Stews

Ingredients:

- 1 tablespoon Olive Oil
- 1 Small White Onion, chopped
- 2 tablespoons Fresh Ginger, chopped
- 4 Large Carrots, peeled and chopped
- 1 Apple, peeled, cored, and chopped
- 8 ounces Canned Chickpeas, no added salt
- 3 teaspoons Ground Cinnamon

- 4 cups Vegetable Broth, no added salt
- 1.5 cups Unsweetened Plain Almond Milk

Directions:

1. In a large pot over medium heat, heat the olive oil. Add the onion and ginger. Cook until the onion is soft and translucent, approximately 5 minutes.
2. Add the carrots, apple, chickpeas, cinnamon, and broth.
3. Simmer the soup until the vegetables are tender, about 15 minutes.
4. Remove from heat and pour the soup into a blender. Add the almond milk and blend until smooth. Alternatively, use an immersion blender and blend the vegetables and almond milk in the pot until smooth.

Tip: *Elevate your culinary adventure by introducing 1 teaspoon of turmeric and 1 teaspoon of curry powder for an extra kick.*

Savory Snack Mix

Meal Type: Appetizers & snacks | Serving Size: ½ cup

Ingredients:

- 6 tablespoons margarine
- 2 tablespoons Worcestershire sauce
- 1½ teaspoons seasoning salt
- ¾ teaspoon garlic powder

- ½ teaspoon onion powder
- 3 cups Crispix
- 3 cups Cheerios
- 3 cups Corn Flakes
- 1 cup Kix
- 1 cup Pretzels
- 1 cup Bagel Chips, broken into 1-inch pieces

Directions:

1. Heat oven to 250 degrees Fahrenheit.
2. Melt margarine in a large roasting pan in the oven. Stir in seasonings. Continuously blend in the remaining components until they are uniformly distributed.
3. Allow to cook for 60 minutes, agitating at 15-minute intervals. Spread on paper towels to cool. Store in an airtight container.

Aromatic Basmati Rice and Seasonal Fresh Herbs

Meal Type: Main Dish | Serving Size: ⅙

Ingredients:

- 1½ cups basmati rice
- 2 tablespoons margarine
- 2 cups chopped sweet onions (Vidalia)
- 2 ½ cups low sodium chicken stock or water
- 3 tablespoons finely chopped flat-leafed parsley

- 2 tablespoons finely chopped dill
- 2 tablespoons finely chopped tarragon

Directions:

1. Wash the rice with cold water repeatedly until the water becomes transparent, then put it aside.
2. Melt margarine in a large saucepan over medium-high heat and sauté onions until translucent, about 5 minutes.
3. Add rice, 2½ cups of stock, or water and bring to a boil.
4. Reduce heat to low, cover, and cook until rice is tender, about 15 minutes. Take off the stove and allow it to rest, covered, for ten minutes.
5. Stir in herbs and season with pepper.

Double Cranberry Pear Crisp

Meal Type: Desserts & sweets | Serving Size: 172 g

Ingredients:

TOPPING

- ¾ cup quick-cooking rolled oats
- 2 tbsp. whole-wheat flour
- ¼ cup brown sugar
- 2 tbsp. chopped, toasted nuts
- 1 tsp. cinnamon
- 2 tbsp. soft, non-hydrogenated margarine

FILLING

- 3 mature pears, peeled, seeds extracted, & finely cut
- 1½cups fresh or frozen cranberries (if frozen, do not defrost)
- ½ cup chopped, dried cranberries
- ½ cup brown sugar
- 1 tbsp. all-purpose flour

Preparation:

1. Preheat the oven to 375°F.
2. Prepare an 8″ x 8″ ovenproof dish by spraying with vegetable oil cooking spray.
3. Combine oats, whole wheat flour, brown sugar, nuts, and cinnamon in a bowl and mix well. Utilize a fork or your fingertips to incorporate the margarine into the dry ingredients until they become sufficiently moistened. Set aside.
4. In the prepared baking dish, combine pears and cranberries. Mix the fruit thoroughly with brown sugar and flour to ensure an even coating. Sprinkle the oatmeal mixture evenly over the fruit.
5. Bake for about 40 minutes, or until the fruit is soft and the topping is golden brown.

Peach Raspberry Smoothie

Meal Type: Breakfasts & brunch | Serving Size: 1 cup smoothie

Ingredients:

- 1 cup frozen raspberries
- 1 medium peach, pit removed, sliced
- ½ cup tofu
- 1 tablespoon of either honey/sweetener (such as stevia or Splenda)
- 1 cup unfortified almond milk

Directions:

Blend all components until a smooth consistency is achieved.

Eggplant & Chickpea Bites

Meal Type: Appetizers & snacks | Serving Size: ½ |

Ingredients:

- 3 large eggplants/aubergines, halved, cut side scored
- Cooking spray oil
- 2 large garlic cloves, peeled
- 2 tsp coriander
- 2 tsp cumin seeds
- 400g canned chickpeas, drained & rinsed
- 2 tbsp chickpea flour
- ½ lemon zested and juice

- ½ lemon cut into wedges to serve
- 3 tbsp polenta

Directions:

1. Heat oven to 200C/180C fan/gas 6. Coat/spray the halves of eggplant with oil, and arrange them in a sizable roasting pan, flesh-side facing upwards, along with the garlic, coriander, and cumin seeds. Season, then roast for 40 minutes until the eggplant is completely tender. Set aside to cool a little.
2. Scoop the eggplant flesh into a bowl and discard the skins. Use a spatula to scrape the spices and garlic into the bowl. Combine the garbanzo beans, garbanzo bean flour, grated lemon peel, and lemon juice, then coarsely crush the ingredients. Season to taste. The consistency may appear somewhat loose, but it will solidify once refrigerated.
3. Form the blend into 20 balls and arrange them on a parchment paper-covered baking sheet. Refrigerate for a minimum of 30 minutes to set.
4. Heat oven to 180C/160C fan/gas 4. Tip the polenta onto a plate, roll the balls in it to coat, then return them to the tray and spray each one with a little oil. Roast for 20 mins until crisp, hot, and golden. Serve with

lemon wedges on the side. The recipe also pairs well with harissa yogurt dip.

Roasted Red Pepper & Chickpea Hummus

Meal Type: Dips & spreads

Ingredients:

- 3 large eggplants/aubergines, halved, cut side scored
- Cooking spray oil
- 2 large garlic cloves, peeled
- 2 tsp coriander
- 2 tsp cumin seeds
- 400g canned chickpeas, drained & rinsed
- 2 tbsp chickpea flour
- ½ lemon zested and juice
- ½ lemon cut into wedges to serve
- 3 tbsp polenta

Directions:

1. Heat oven to 200C/180C fan/gas 6. Coat the halved eggplants with oil and arrange them in a spacious roasting pan, cut side facing upwards, accompanied by the garlic, coriander, and cumin seeds. Season, then roast for 40 minutes until the eggplant is completely tender. Set aside to cool a little.

2. Scoop the eggplant flesh into a bowl and discard the skins. Use a spatula to scrape the spices and garlic into the bowl. Incorporate the chickpeas, besan, and both the zest and juice of the lemon into the mixture, then coarsely crush them. Season to taste. The mixture may appear somewhat loose, but it will solidify upon refrigeration.
3. Proceed to form the blend into 20 balls and arrange them on a parchment paper-lined baking sheet. Refrigerate for a minimum of 30 minutes to set.
4. Heat oven to 180C/160C fan/gas 4. Tip the polenta onto a plate, roll the balls in it to coat, then return them to the tray and spray each one with a little oil. Roast for 20 mins until crisp, hot, and golden. Serve with lemon wedges on the side. The recipe also pairs well with harissa yogurt dip.

Zucchini-Carrot Soup

Meal Type: Soups & stews

Ingredients:

- 1 medium onion, finely diced
- 2 cloves of garlic, minced
- 2 cups veggie broth, no salt added
- 2 cups oat milk
- 3 tablespoons coarsely ground oat flour

- 1 teaspoon basil
- ½ teaspoon oregano
- 2 small zucchinis, grated
- 1 medium carrot, grated
- Mrs. Dash spices and Bragg's Aminos liquid/shakes

Directions:

1. In a large saucepan, sauté the onion and garlic in a little water or broth until tender.
2. Stir in broth and milk and bring to a boil.
3. Whisk in coarsely ground oat flour, basil, oregano, and a couple of shakes of Mrs. Dash.
4. Add zucchini and carrots.
5. Reduce heat and cook for 5 minutes until veggies are tender. Stir often so the soup doesn't scorch.
6. Add a few shakes of Bragg's Aminos and enjoy.

Tomato-Lentil Delight

Ingredients:

- 1 tablespoon of olive oil
- 1 medium-sized onion
- 2 carrots (about 100g)
- 3 garlic cloves
- 2 stalks of celery
- 100g dried red lentils

- 400g canned tomatoes
- 2 tablespoons of tomato puree
- 2 tablespoons of balsamic vinegar
- 1 tablespoon of dried basil
- 1 low-salt vegetable stock cube
- 400ml boiling water
- 240g dried pasta

Instructions:

1. Begin by peeling the onion, garlic, and carrots. Proceed to dice all the vegetables into small, evenly-sized pieces.
2. In a large pan set to low heat, add the olive oil. Introduce the diced onion, garlic, carrot, and celery, and gently heat. Stir regularly for approximately 10 minutes until the vegetables are tender.
3. Prepare the stock by dissolving the low-salt stock cube in 400ml of boiling water.
4. Add the dried lentils, canned tomatoes, dried basil, tomato puree, stock, and balsamic vinegar to the pan. Simmer for about 20 minutes.
5. For the pasta, bring a generously filled saucepan of water to a boil. Add the desired pasta and cook according to the package instructions.
6. Once the pasta is cooked, drain it and serve with the Tomato-Lentil Delight.

Savory Roasted Cabbage Wedges

Ingredients:

- 1 head of green cabbage, sliced into 1-inch wedges
- 2 teaspoons of sugar
- ¼ teaspoon of freshly ground pepper (adjust to taste)
- 1 tablespoon of balsamic vinegar
- 2 tablespoons of olive oil

Instructions:

1. Preheat your oven and a baking sheet to 450°F.
2. In a small bowl, combine the sugar and freshly ground pepper.
3. Quarter the cabbage through the core and then cut each quarter into 1-inch wedges, ensuring the core is intact to maintain the structure of the wedges.
4. Brush the cabbage wedges with olive oil and sprinkle them with the sugar and pepper mixture.
5. Place the seasoned cabbage wedges on the hot baking sheet and roast until they become tender and develop a light golden brown color around the edges, approximately 25 minutes.
6. Drizzle the roasted cabbage with balsamic vinegar.

Easy and Light-Tasting Coleslaw

Serving size: ½ cup

Ingredients:

Salad:

- 1 head cabbage, shredded or chopped
- 1 carrot, grated

Dressing:

- ⅓ cup white vinegar (or try with half white vinegar and half apple cider or raspberry vinegar)
- ⅓ cup white sugar
- ⅓ cup canola oil (or less)
- 1 tsp celery seed

Directions:

1. In a small saucepan, bring the dressing ingredients to a boil on high heat while stirring constantly.
2. Remove from heat and pour over prepared vegetables.
3. Toss to mix, cover, and refrigerate.
4. The salad is best if made early in the day or the night before and keeps well.

Roasted Cabbage Wedges

Ingredients:

- 1 green cabbage (cut into 1" wedges)
- 2 tsp sugar

- ¼ teaspoon of freshly ground black pepper (adjust according to taste preference)
- 1 tbsp balsamic vinegar
- 2 tbsp olive oil

Directions:

1. Preheat the oven and baking sheet to 450°F.
2. Combine pepper and sugar in a small bowl.
3. Quarter cabbage through the core and cut each quarter into 1-inch wedges, trying to leave the core intact to prevent the cabbage wedges from falling apart.
4. Brush wedges with oil and sprinkle with sugar and pepper.
5. Place the seasoned wedges on the hot baking sheet and roast until cabbage is tender and lightly browned around the edges, about 25 minutes.
6. Drizzle cabbage with balsamic vinegar.

Butternut Bliss Pasta Bake

Ingredients:

- 1 butternut squash (approx. 600g)
- 175ml full-fat coconut milk
- 2 teaspoons Dijon mustard
- 1 low-salt vegetable stock cube
- 1 teaspoon cider vinegar
- 250g macaroni pasta

- Black pepper
- 100g breadcrumbs
- 50g vegan grated cheese
- 30g flaked almonds
- 1 tablespoon fresh parsley (optional)
- 200g broccoli

Instructions:

1. Preheat the oven to 160°C/gas mark 5. Halve and deseed a butternut squash. Place the squash halves flesh side down in a roasting tin and pour in 200ml water. Place in the oven and cook for ninety minutes.
2. Allow the squash to cool slightly before scooping out the flesh with a spoon. Add the squash to a blender with the coconut milk to create a smooth puree.
3. Once pureed, heat gently in a saucepan. Add Dijon mustard, and cider vinegar, and crumble in the stock cube. Season with pepper and add a little water to the sauce if needed. Simmer for 20 minutes until it thickens.
4. Heat a substantial pot of water until it reaches a boiling point. Add the macaroni and allow it to simmer for seven minutes, keeping in mind that it will undergo further cooking during the baking process. Drain the pasta and combine with the sauce, pouring them into an ovenproof dish.

5. Combine the breadcrumbs, almonds, vegan cheese, and parsley if using. Scatter atop the pasta and place in the oven to cook for 10 minutes, or until a golden brown hue is achieved.
6. Bring a saucepan of water to the boil and add the broccoli. Cook until tender, drain, and serve with the Butternut Bliss Pasta Bake.

Mediterranean Bean and Couscous Salad

Ingredients:

- 1 tablespoon olive oil
- 1 red onion, finely chopped
- 150g couscous
- 240ml low-salt vegetable stock
- 1 red pepper, chopped into 1cm pieces
- 400g in three bean salad, in water
- 10g fresh parsley, chopped (optional)

Instructions:

1. Chop the onion and pepper and set aside.
2. Make the vegetable stock and measure the couscous. Stir the hot vegetable stock into the couscous, cover, and leave to sit for five minutes.

3. Heat the olive oil in a small pan. Sauté the onion on low heat for five minutes or until soft, then remove the pan from the heat.
4. Uncover the couscous and use a fork to fluff it up. Add the cooked onion and fresh pepper, then drain the bean salad and add to the couscous. Stir gently until well mixed. If using parsley, sprinkle it over the salad before serving.

Spicy Black Bean Tacos with Roasted Vegetables

Ingredients:

- 1 red onion, cut into thin strips
- 1 red pepper, cut into thin strips
- 2 tablespoons olive oil
- 200g tin of sweetcorn in water
- ½ teaspoon smoked paprika
- 400g tin black beans in water
- 2 garlic cloves, grated
- ½ teaspoon ground cinnamon
- ½ teaspoon ground cumin
- Black pepper
- 50g cherry tomatoes, quartered
- 1 spring onion, thinly sliced
- 5g fresh coriander, chopped
- ¼ teaspoon hot chili sauce

- 2 limes
- 1 small avocado, ripe
- 8 mini tortilla wraps
- 1 fresh chili, thinly sliced (optional)

Instructions:

1. Preheat the oven to 180°C/gas mark 4 and line two baking trays with greaseproof paper. Put the sliced onion and red pepper into a bowl. Add a tablespoon of oil, season with pepper to taste, and blend thoroughly. Arrange the seasoned vegetables evenly across one of the baking sheets.
2. Drain the sweetcorn and pat it dry. Pour it into a bowl, season with pepper and the smoked paprika, and stir to combine. Spread the sweetcorn onto the second baking tray. Insert both pans into the oven and bake for 25 to 30 minutes. Halfway through the baking process, give them a thorough mix. Afterwards, set aside to allow for cooling.
3. Drain and rinse the beans, pour into a bowl, and mash with a fork. Heat the oil in a saucepan on medium heat and add the garlic. Stir for 30 secs, then add the cinnamon, cumin, black pepper, black beans, and a little water if needed.

4. Cook gently for three minutes, then remove from the heat. For the salsa, put the chili sauce in a bowl and squeeze in the juice of ½ a lime, mix. Add the diced tomatoes, chopped spring onions, and fresh coriander leaves, then blend thoroughly.
5. For the guacamole, halve the avocado and carefully remove the stone. Scoop all the avocado flesh into another bowl, squeeze in the juice of one lime, and mash with a fork to a creamy texture. Set aside until serving.
6. Lay out the tortilla wraps. Place a layer of black beans, assorted vegetables, and corn atop each one, then garnish with a small amount of salsa and guacamole. Serve two tacos per person, with a wedge of lime (and the chili and extra chopped coriander if desired).

Vegan Gluten-Free White Bread

Ingredients:

- 6 tablespoons chickpea flour (gram flour)
- 400ml water
- 6 tablespoons vegetable oil
- 1 tablespoon cider vinegar
- 2 tablespoons sugar
- 6 tablespoons water
- 500g gluten-free bread flour

- 7g fast-action yeast
- Oil for greasing

Instructions:

1. Oil a non-stick 1kg loaf tin. Mix the chickpea flour with the six tablespoons of water until you have a thick and creamy mixture.
2. In a bowl, whisk together the chickpea flour mix, three tablespoons of oil, cider vinegar, sugar, and 400ml of water.
3. Gradually add in the gluten-free bread flour and yeast, stirring to make a thick batter. Pour over the remaining three tablespoons of oil and lightly stir into the batter. Avoid over-mixing.
4. Turn out the dough into the oiled loaf tin and smooth the top with your hand. Loosely cover with oiled cling film.
5. Set aside somewhere warm for 1 hour and 30 minutes to allow the dough to rise to the top of the tin. Preheat the oven to 220°C/gas mark 6.
6. Bake for 55-60 minutes until the bread has risen and is golden brown. Once done, take it out of the oven, carefully turn out the loaf onto a wire rack, and cool before slicing it into 10 portions.

Plant-Based Indian-Inspired Stuffed Peppers

Ingredients:

- 120g red lentils, dried
- 1 tablespoon vegetable oil
- 1 onion, finely chopped
- 2 garlic cloves, crushed or finely chopped
- 1cm fresh ginger, grated or finely chopped
- 1 teaspoon tomato puree
- 1 teaspoon ground cumin
- 1 teaspoon garam masala
- 200g basmati rice
- 1 low-salt vegetable stock cube
- 850ml boiling water
- 20g fresh mint leaves
- 8 peppers (red, yellow, or orange)

Instructions:

1. Preheat the oven to 200°C/gas mark 6. Wash the dried lentils, drain, and set aside.
2. Heat the oil in a large saucepan. Add the onion, garlic, and ginger, then gently cook on low heat for 5 minutes until softened. Stir in the tomato puree and spices, and cook for an additional 1 minute.
3. Add the rice, and stir well to coat in the flavors. Dissolve the vegetable stock cube in

boiling water and pour it over the rice. Bring to a boil, then add the lentils.

4. Cover the saucepan with a lid and let it cook over low heat for 15 minutes until the lentils and rice are cooked. Roughly chop and stir in the mint.
5. Slice the tops off the peppers, remove the middle stalk, and scoop out the seeds. Trim the bottoms of the peppers to ensure they stand upright.
6. Carefully fill each pepper with the mixture and place the lid on top. Bake in the oven for 25-30 minutes or until the peppers have softened and begun to color. Serve two per person.

Red Velvet Loaf Cake

Ingredients:

For the cake:

- 200ml dairy-free milk, unsweetened
- 4 teaspoons cider vinegar
- 200g gluten-free plain flour
- ½ teaspoon xanthan gum
- 150g caster sugar
- 2 tablespoons cocoa powder
- ¼ teaspoon baking powder
- ¼ teaspoon bicarbonate of soda
- Red food coloring (as needed)

For the icing:

- 50g dairy-free butter
- 65g dairy-free cream cheese
- ½ tsp vanilla extract
- 350g icing sugar

Instructions:

1. Mix the dairy-free milk with the cider vinegar and set aside for 10 minutes.
2. Preheat the oven to 180°C/gas mark 4. Grease and line a 450g loaf tin.
3. In a large metal bowl, combine the gluten-free flour, xanthan gum, caster sugar, cocoa powder, baking powder, and bicarbonate of soda. Mix by hand until fully combined.
4. Add the milk and vinegar mix, oil, and red food coloring to the dry ingredients. Using a metal spoon, quickly mix everything until combined, dissolving any small lumps.
5. Spoon the batter into the loaf tin and bake for 30 minutes or until a skewer comes out clean. Place the tin on a wire rack for 10 minutes, then remove the cake and let it cool completely.
6. To make the icing, beat together dairy-free butter, cream cheese, vanilla extract, and icing sugar until thick enough to spread or

pipe. Adjust consistency with a little dairy-free milk if needed.

7. Once the cake is cold, ice it with the cream cheese frosting. Slice and serve.

Rice Pudding with Pear and Prune Compote

Ingredients:

- 300g pudding rice
- 1200ml organic soya milk
- 410g tin prunes in juice
- 410g tin pears in juice
- 1 lemon
- ½ teaspoon ground ginger

Instructions:

1. In a large saucepan, combine soya milk and rice. Stir while bringing it to a boil. Reduce the heat and simmer for 20 minutes or until the rice is soft.
2. Stir occasionally, scraping the bottom of the pot to remove any stuck rice.
3. Drain the juice from the tinned prunes and pears, discarding the juice. Put the fruit into a saucepan with ground ginger. Slice the lemon and squeeze its juice, incorporating it into the fruit mixture.

4. Heat the fruit until it breaks down into a thick sauce.
5. Once the rice is cooked, serve the rice pudding with a tablespoon of the fruit compote on top.

Rooh Afza Lemonade

Meal Type: Juice | Serving Size: 2 | Prep Time: 5 mins |

Ingredients:

- 500ml water, chilled
- 2 tablespoons Rooh Afza syrup
- 2 tablespoons lemon juice
- 1 tablespoon sugar
- Handful of mint leaves
- Ice cubes

Instructions:

1. In a jug, combine chilled water, Rooh Afza syrup, lemon juice, sugar, mint leaves, and ice cubes.
2. Stir the mixture thoroughly until a uniform consistency is achieved with all components fully integrated.
3. Serve this refreshing Rooh Afza lemonade chilled, perfect for a special occasion or to enjoy after a long day.

Fresh Zippy Strawberry Salad

Ingredients:

Dressing:

- ½ cup vegetable oil
- ⅓ cup white wine vinegar
- 1 garlic clove, minced
- 2 tbsp. brown sugar
- 1 tsp. curry powder
- 1 tsp. soy sauce (low sodium)

Salad:

- 10 cups torn salad greens
- ½ cup slivered almonds, toasted
- 1 cup grapes (red/green), halved
- 2 cups sliced strawberries
- ½ cup crushed, unsalted pretzels
- 2 cups mandarin orange segments

Directions:

1. Combine all dressing ingredients and shake well. Set aside.
2. Combine mixed greens and strawberries with the dressing.
3. Sprinkle it with almonds and pretzels. Serve immediately.

Cucumber Salad

Ingredients:

- 3 English cucumbers, peeled or striped

- 1 red onion
- ½ cup rice vinegar
- ½ cup water
- ⅓ cup sugar
- 2 tablespoons of white toasted sesame seeds, for garnish

Directions:

1. Thinly cut the cucumber into circular pieces and chop up the red onion into tiny cubes, then toss them together in a mixing bowl.
2. Stir together rice vinegar, water, and sugar and pour over cucumber and onion.
3. Cover and marinate for an hour.
4. Plate and garnish with sesame seeds.

Curried Eggplant Mix

Meal Type: Dip Appetizers & Snacks

Ingredients:

- 1 medium eggplant (roasted)
- 1 tbsp lemon juice
- 2 cloves garlic
- 2 tsp curry powder
- ¼ tsp ginger
- ¼ cup fresh cilantro

Directions:

1. Slice eggplants in half and score.

2. Drizzle with olive oil and roast at 350°F until the flesh becomes soft (45-60 minutes).
3. Scoop out the flesh and discard skins.
4. Combine all ingredients in a food processor until smooth.
5. Serve with baked pita chips.

The Green Beans Garlic Salad Veggies

Ingredients:

- 2 cups green beans
- 2 cloves garlic, chopped
- 1 tbsp balsamic or red wine vinegar
- 1 tbsp sesame oil

Directions:

1. Clean the beans and cook in boiling water until tender.
2. Drain and cool under cold water.
3. Toss the beans with the garlic, vinegar, and oil.

Fragrant Basmati Rice Grains & Pasta

Ingredients:

- 1 cup white basmati rice

- 2 tsp olive oil
- 1 bay leaf
- ½ tsp turmeric
- ¼ tsp cardamom
- 1 cinnamon stick
- 1½ cups water

Directions:

1. Heat oil in a saucepan.
2. Add the rice and spices to the pan and toast slightly.
3. Pour in the water and heat it until it starts bubbling.
4. Reduce heat, cover, and simmer for approximately 15 minutes.

Vegan Herbs Pasta

Ingredients:

- 1 lb white spaghetti or linguine
- ½ cup extra virgin olive oil
- 2 cloves of garlic, minced
- Black pepper (to taste)
- 1 tsp dry chili flakes
- 1 green onion
- ½ cup of freshly cut herbs (like basil and oregano), finely chopped

Directions:

1. Cook pasta according to directions.

2. In a skillet, sauté garlic, pepper, chili flakes, and onion in olive oil.
3. Add cooked pasta and fresh herbs to the oil.
4. Toss together and serve immediately.

Zucchini Corn Sauté Sandwiches & Wraps

Ingredients:

- 2 medium zucchinis, diced
- 2 cups frozen corn
- 1 medium sweet red pepper, diced
- 1 tsp red chili flakes
- 1 tbsp vegetable oil

Directions:

1. Heat oil in a pan.
2. Add vegetables and chili, and cook on high heat until zucchini becomes tender.

Roasted Red Pepper Coulis

Ingredients:

- 1 cup roasted red peppers
- ¼ cup extra virgin olive oil
- 2 tbsp lemon juice
- 1 garlic clove, minced

Directions:

1. Pure all ingredients in a blender.

2. Add herbs to taste.

Lemony Orzo Salad

Ingredients:

- 1 cup orzo pasta
- 1 red pepper, diced
- 1 green onion, diced
- 2 tbsp tarragon, chopped
- 2 tbsp parsley, chopped
- 2 tbsp lemon juice
- 1 tsp garlic, minced
- 1 tbsp extra virgin olive oil
- ½ tsp black pepper

Directions:

1. Cook orzo in boiling water for 8 to 10 minutes (or cook pasta of choice according to cook times labeled on the box).
2. Drain and cool under running water.
3. Add remaining ingredients and serve.

Asian Eggplant Dip

Ingredients:

- 1 large eggplant
- 2 tbsp brown sugar
- 1 tbsp rice vinegar
- 1 tbsp water

- 1 tsp vegetable oil
- 4 cloves garlic, finely chopped
- 1 tbsp finely chopped fresh ginger root
- 4 green onions, chopped
- 1 tsp chili paste
- 1 tsp sesame oil
- 2 tbsp chopped fresh cilantro

Directions:

1. Roast eggplant in a preheated 425°F oven for approximately 45 minutes.
2. Peel eggplant and chop finely.
3. In a small bowl, combine sugar, vinegar, and water.
4. In a large skillet, sauté garlic, ginger, green onions, and chili paste until fragrant.
5. Add vinegar mixture.
6. When bubbling, add eggplant.
7. Stir to combine.
8. Remove from heat and add sesame oil and fresh chopped cilantro.
9. Serve cold or at room temperature.

Easy Pear and Arugula Salad

Ingredients:

- ⅔ cup extra virgin olive oil
- 1 shallot, minced
- 3 tbsp red wine vinegar
- Cracked black pepper

- 1 tsp Dijon mustard
- 6 cups of arugula, cleaned and with stems removed.
- 1 pear, sliced

Directions:

1. In a blender, combine all ingredients except oil, arugula, and pear.
2. Slowly add oil to emulsify.
3. Mix the salad components and gently coat them with the dressing.
4. Try serving it with garlic ricotta crostini.

Easy Tarragon Dressing with Salad

Ingredients:

- 1 tsp Dijon mustard
- 2 tbsp lemon juice
- 2 tbsp white wine vinegar
- 1 tbsp minced shallot
- 2 tbsp fresh tarragon or 1 tsp dried tarragon
- ⅓ cup extra virgin olive oil
- 8 cups mixed greens or lettuce

Directions:

1. Mince shallots.
2. Add mustard, tarragon, lemon juice, and vinegar.
3. Whisk in olive oil.
4. Drizzle over greens.

Tasty Double Boiled Mashed Potatoes

Ingredients:

- 4 small potatoes
- Water
- 1 tablespoon of unsalted safflower oil margarine

Directions:

1. Peel the potatoes.
2. Cut into strips (1.2 cm x 1.2 cm) or dice (2 cm x 2 cm x 2 cm).
3. Boil in water (1.5 L) for 8 minutes.
4. Drain potatoes.
5. Add clean water (1.5 liters) and soak for 12 hours.
6. Use as required, e.g., mash, potato salad, home fries, baked.
7. Add 1 tablespoon of unsalted margarine to reheated potatoes and mash with water until the desired consistency is achieved.

Sweet Cauliflower with Fresh Dill

Ingredients:

- 1 medium head of cauliflower
- 2 tbsp (25 mL) lemon juice
- 1 tbsp (15 mL) olive oil

- ⅓ cup (75 mL) fresh dill, chopped
- Pepper to taste

Directions:

1. Remove leaves and stems from cauliflower; cut into florets.
2. Cook in a large pot of boiling water, covered for 10 minutes or until tender; drain.
3. Transfer to a serving dish.
4. Mix lemon juice with oil; pour over cauliflower and stir to mix.
5. Sprinkle with dill, and add pepper to taste.

Warm Mushroom Salad with Watercress

Meal type: Salads/Side dish

Ingredients:

- 4 tbsp olive oil
- 2 tbsp balsamic vinegar
- ½ tsp thyme
- 1 cup assorted mushrooms
- ½ cup shallots
- 4 cups of mixed greens (including watercress)

Directions:

1. Saute mushrooms and shallots in olive oil.
2. Season with thyme and finish with balsamic vinegar.

3. Serve over a bed of greens.

Delicious Asian Apple Slaw

Meal Type: Salads

Ingredients:

- 4 cups of cabbage, finely shredded
- ½ cup red pepper, chopped
- 3 green onions, chopped
- 1 granny smith apple, shredded
- ½ cup celery, chopped
- ½ cup cilantro
- 2 tbsp toasted sesame seeds
- ½ cup vegetable oil
- 1 tsp sesame oil
- ¼ cup lime juice
- ¼ cup rice wine vinegar
- 2 tbsp sugar/Splenda

Directions:

1. Combine all fresh herbs, fruit, and vegetables in a large mixing bowl.
2. In a separate bowl, whisk together oils, lime juice, vinegar, and sugar.
3. Mix the slaw with the salad dressing and sprinkle toasted sesame seeds on top as a garnish.

Tasty Ghanouj Delight Dip

Meal Type: Appetizers & Snacks

Ingredients:

- 1 large eggplant, halved lengthwise
- 1 whole garlic head, unpeeled
- 2 tablespoons (30 ml) olive oil
- Lemon juice, to taste

Directions:

1. Begin by preheating the oven to 350°F and lining a baking sheet with parchment paper.
2. Place the halved eggplant, cut side down, on the prepared baking sheet. Roast until the flesh becomes extremely tender and easily separates from the skin. This typically takes about 1 hour, depending on the size of the eggplant. Allow it to cool.
3. Trim the tips off the garlic cloves. Wrap the cloves in a piece of aluminum foil, sealing it tightly. Roast the garlic alongside the eggplant until it turns tender, approximately 20 minutes. Allow it to cool, then press the roasted garlic through a garlic press to create a purée.
4. Scoop out the softened flesh from the eggplant using a spoon and transfer it to a food processor. Add the garlic purée, olive oil, and lemon juice. Process the mixture

until it achieves a smooth consistency. Season with pepper to taste.

5. Serve this delightful Eggplant Delight Dip with mini pitas for a flavorful and satisfying snack.

Fruity Oat Crisp Delight

Meal Type: Desserts & Sweets

Ingredients:

Crisp;

- 1¼ cups (310 ml) quick-cooking rolled oats
- ¼ cup (60 ml) brown sugar
- ¼ cup (60 ml) unbleached all-purpose flour
- 6 tablespoons (90 ml) non-hydrogenated margarine, melted

Filling;

- ½ cup (125 ml) brown sugar
- 4 teaspoons (20 ml) cornstarch
- 4 cups fresh or frozen blueberries (not thawed)
- 2 cups (500 ml) grated or chopped apples
- 1 tablespoon (15 ml) margarine, melted
- 1 tablespoon (15 ml) lemon juice

Directions:

1. Preheat the oven to 350°F with the rack in the middle position.

2. In a bowl, combine the dry ingredients for the crisp. Add melted margarine and stir until just moistened. Set aside.
3. In an 8-inch square baking dish, combine brown sugar and cornstarch for the filling. Add fruits, and lemon juice, and toss to combine.
4. Top the fruit mixture with the crisp mixture and bake for 55 minutes to 1 hour or until the crisp turns golden brown.
5. Serve this Fruity Oat Crisp Delight either warm or cold, making it an excellent choice for a picnic, BBQ, or any summer celebration.

Savory Roasted Red Pepper Delight

Meal Type: Appetizers & Snacks

Ingredients:

- 1 cup roasted red peppers
- 1 tbsp olive oil
- 1 tsp lemon juice
- 1 clove garlic
- 1 tsp cumin

Directions:

1. Mix all the ingredients in a food processor until well combined.

2. Serve this delightful Roasted Red Pepper Dip with baked pita chips for a tasty and kidney-friendly snack.

Garlicky Swiss Chard Bliss

Meal Type: Side Dish | Serving size: 1 or 2 |

Ingredients:

- 1 large bunch of Swiss chard (about 100 g)
- 1 tbsp olive oil
- 2 garlic cloves, minced
- ¼ tsp red chili flakes
- 1 tbsp balsamic vinegar or lemon juice

Directions:

1. Clean the Swiss chard leaves and remove the stems.
2. Heat olive oil in a skillet, add minced garlic and red chili flakes.
3. Toss Swiss chard leaves over high heat until wilted.
4. Add balsamic vinegar or lemon juice. Serve with cracked pepper.

Savory Tofu Fingers Delight

Meal Type: Main Course

Ingredients:

- 1 tsp tamari sauce

- 2 tbsp water
- ½ cup cornflake crumbs
- 1 teaspoon of seasoning (such as garlic powder, curry powder, paprika, or another spice of your choice)
- 1 ½ cups (12 oz) firm tofu

Directions:

1. Combine tamari sauce and water in a small bowl.
2. In another bowl, mix cornflake crumbs and seasoning.
3. Dip tofu into the tamari-water mixture, then into the seasoned crumbs.
4. Place tofu slices on a baking sheet, and lightly wipe them with vegetable oil.
5. Bake at 350°F for 20 minutes, flipping once to brown both sides.

Zesty Pina Colada Smoothie

Meal Type: | Beverages, Breakfasts & Brunch | Servings for 1 or 2 |

Ingredients:

- 1 cup pineapple, canned or fresh
- 1 cup (8 oz) firm tofu
- ½ cup unsweetened pineapple juice
- 1 tsp Stevia or other sweetener
- 1 pinch of red pepper flakes

Directions:

- Puree all the ingredients in a blender.
- Serve and Enjoy.

Icy Smoothie

Meal Type: Beverage & Breakfast| Serving Size: 4 |

Ingredients:

- 2 cups soft silken tofu
- 3 cups ice
- 2 tablespoons of either coffee powder or green tea powder
- 2 teaspoons vanilla extract
- 2 Tablespoons rice syrup

Preparation:

Put all the ingredients into a blender and blend until the mixture is smooth and has a thick consistency.

Spicy Hot Cereal

Meal Type: Snack & Appetizer| Serving Size: ¼ |

Ingredients:

- 4 cups of water
- 2 cups of cream of rice or any other hot rice cereal, grits, or Cream of Wheat
- 1 teaspoon of vanilla extract
- ¼ cup of maple syrup

- 1 teaspoon of powdered ginger

Instructions:

1. Heat the water in a medium-sized pot until it reaches a boiling point.
2. Gradually whisk in the cereal and reduce the heat. Continue to stir the mixture until it achieves a smooth consistency.
3. Lower the heat to simmer and add the remaining ingredients while stirring.
4. Let it cook, stirring occasionally, until you achieve your desired texture.

Lemon Hummus

Serving Size: Makes 1 pint

Ingredients:

- 2 cups cooked garbanzo beans
- ⅓ cup tahini
- ¼ cup lemon juice
- 2 minced garlic cloves
- 1 Tablespoon olive oil
- ½ teaspoon paprika
- 1 teaspoon parsley flakes

Preparation:

1. Combine garbanzo beans, tahini, lemon juice, and garlic in a blender or food processor.
2. Blend until the mixture is smooth.
3. Transfer the mixture to a serving bowl.

4. Drizzle olive oil over the top, then sprinkle with paprika and parsley.
5. Serve with pita triangles or unsalted crackers.

Corn and Cilantro Salsa

Meal Type: Lunch| Serving Size: Serves 6-8 |

Ingredients:

- 3 cups fresh white or yellow corn cut from the cob
- ½ cup chopped cilantro
- 1 cup of diced sweet onions (like Vidalia or Maui onions)
- ½ cup chopped fresh tomato
- 4 Tablespoons lemon or lime juice
- ¼ teaspoon dried oregano
- 2 teaspoons chili powder or red pepper flakes

Preparation:

1. Place corn in a medium-sized bowl.
2. Add remaining ingredients and mix well.
3. Cover the mixture and place it in the refrigerator for at least one hour before serving.

Renal Mushroom Pockets

Meal Type: Main Course | Serving Size: Serves 6 |

Ingredients:

- 2 Tablespoons water
- 2 Tablespoons lemon or lime juice
- 1 Tablespoon vegetable oil
- 2 minced garlic cloves
- 1 teaspoon ground cumin
- 1 teaspoon crushed dried oregano
- 3 cups of thinly sliced fresh mushrooms, such as portobello caps, brown crimini, or white button mushrooms
- 1 cup thinly sliced bell pepper
- ½ cup chopped scallions (white parts only)
- 3 Tablespoons shredded vegan soy cheese
- Six 7-inch flour tortillas

Preparation Instructions:

1. In a large bowl, combine water, juice, oil, garlic, cumin, and oregano, and mix well. Add mushrooms, peppers, and scallions. Stir to coat. Allow to marinate for at least 30 minutes. If desired, this can be done the day before.
2. Heat a large saucepan. Cook the vegetable mixture with the marinade in a sauté pan until the peppers and scallions become soft, which usually takes around 5-7 minutes. Let

it continue cooking until most of the liquid has evaporated.

3. While the vegetables are cooking, warm the tortillas by either wrapping them in a paper towel and heating them in the microwave or wrapping them in foil and heating them in a 350-degree oven. Place each tortilla on a plate. Spoon on the vegetable mixture and top with cheese.

Fruit Cobbler

Meal Type: Appetizer & Breakfast | Serving Size: Serves 8 |

Ingredients:

- 3 tablespoons melted vegan margarine
- 1 cup all-purpose unbleached flour
- ¼ teaspoon salt
- 1 teaspoon baking powder
- ½ cup rice milk
- 3½ cups pitted fresh cherries
- 1¾ cups white vegan sugar, divided
- 1 tablespoon cornstarch
- 1 cup boiling water

Preparation Instructions:

1. Start by Preheating the oven to 350 degrees Fahrenheit (175 degrees Celsius).
2. Mix melted margarine, flour, salt, baking powder, and rice milk until combined.

3. Toss cherries with ¾ cup sugar and place them in an 8-inch square pan. Cover with dough pieces.
4. Combine remaining sugar and cornstarch. Pour boiling water over the dough. Bake for 35-45 minutes. Serve warm or cold.

Mediterranean Green Beans

(Serving Size: Serves 4, 1 serving = 1 cup)

Ingredients:

- 1 pound fresh green beans, cut
- ¾ cup water
- 2½ teaspoons olive oil
- 3 cloves garlic, minced
- 3 tablespoons lemon juice
- ⅛ teaspoon black pepper

Directions:

1. Boil green beans for 3 minutes; then drain.
2. Sauté garlic and beans in olive oil.
3. Add lemon juice and pepper. Cook for 1 more minute.

Sweet & Crunchy Coleslaw

(Serving Size: Serves 12, 1 serving = ½ cup)

Ingredients:

- 6 cups shredded cabbage

- ½ cup chopped sweet onion
- 1 cup sugar
- 1 cup canola oil
- 1 teaspoon celery seed
- ½ cup rice vinegar
- 1 teaspoon yellow mustard

Directions:

1. Mix cabbage and onion.
2. Blend the remaining ingredients; pour over the cabbage.
3. Refrigerate before serving.

Aromatic Herbed Rice

(Serving Size: **Serves 6, 1 serving = ½ cup)**

Ingredients:

- 3 cups cooked rice
- 2 tablespoons olive oil
- 4–5 cloves garlic, sliced
- 2 tablespoons cilantro, chopped
- 2 tablespoons oregano, chopped
- 2 tablespoons chives, chopped
- ½ teaspoon red pepper flakes
- 1 teaspoon red wine vinegar

Directions:

1. Sauté garlic in olive oil. Add rice, herbs, and pepper flakes; cook for 2–4 minutes.
2. Mix in vinegar; serve.

Pea Salad with Ginger-Lime Vinaigrette

(Serving Size: Serves 6, 1 serving = ½ cup)

Ingredients:

- 1 cup sugar snap peas
- 1 cup snow peas
- 1 cup sweet peas

Vinaigrette:

- 1 tablespoon sesame seeds
- 1 teaspoon reduced-sodium soy sauce
- ¼ cup lime juice
- 1 teaspoon lime zest
- 2 teaspoons ginger, chopped
- ½ cup canola oil
- 1 tablespoon hot sesame oil
- Optional: black pepper

Instructions:

1. Heat a skillet over medium heat and lightly toast the sesame seeds, stirring constantly for about 3–5 minutes.
2. Heat a large pot of water over high heat until it reaches a boiling point. Add all three types of peas and blanch them for 2 minutes. Drain the peas and immediately transfer them to a bowl of cold water to shock them. Once cooled, drain thoroughly using a strainer.

3. In a small bowl, whisk together the soy sauce, lime juice, and lime zest until well-blended, about 1–2 minutes.
4. While whisking continuously, add the chopped ginger. Slowly pour in the canola or grapeseed oil, followed by the sesame oil, and mix until fully incorporated.
5. In a large mixing bowl, combine the salad dressing with the pea mixture. Toss in the toasted sesame seeds and add black pepper to taste.

Tip: *Be mindful of portion sizes as consuming more than one serving can significantly increase potassium intake.*

Plant-Based Apple Oat Delight

Meal Types: Breakfast, Dessert | Prep Time: 10 mins | Cooking Time: 25 mins | Serving Size: 6 |

Ingredients:

- 140g rolled oats
- 1 teaspoon baking powder
- 1 ripe banana
- 100ml plant-based milk (or dairy alternative)
- 1 large flaxseed egg (replace with egg substitute if preferred)
- 2 tablespoons agave syrup (or maple syrup)
- 1 teaspoon vanilla essence

- 2 teaspoons ground cinnamon
- 1 apple, thinly sliced

To Serve:

- 60g non-dairy yogurt
- 10g toasted coconut

Optional:

- 250g stewed fruit (without added sugar) such as pear or apple
- or 400g tinned fruit (tinned in juice, discard the juice), such as peaches or pears

Direction:

1. Preheat the oven to 180°C (356°F) or 160°C (320°F) for fan-assisted ovens, or gas mark 4. Lightly grease an oven-proof dish. Place the oats and baking powder into a blender and blend until finely ground.
2. Add the banana, plant-based milk, flaxseed egg, one tablespoon of syrup, vanilla essence, and ground cinnamon to the blender. Blend until smooth and well combined. Pour the mixture into the prepared oven dish.
3. Coat the sliced apple with the remaining tablespoon of syrup and arrange them over the top of the dish. Bake for 25 minutes.
4. Remove from the oven and let it cool for a few moments. Serve in six portions with a dollop of non-dairy yogurt and a sprinkle of

toasted coconut. Add optional fruit if desired.

Tips:

- This quick and delightful recipe is versatile and perfect for dessert or a special occasion breakfast.
- Adjustments may be needed based on individual kidney diet guidelines; consult your dietitian or doctor for personalized advice.

Plant-Based Vegetable Laksa with Sugar Snap Peas and Pak Choi

Meal Types: Main Meal | Prep Time: 30 minutes | Cooking Time: 25 minutes | Serving Size: 4 |

Ingredients:

Laksa Paste:

- 1 tablespoon vegetable oil
- 2 small shallots, peeled and roughly sliced
- 2 garlic cloves, peeled and chopped
- 1 lemongrass stalk (white part chopped, rest reserved for flavoring)
- 20g ginger (or galangal), peeled and sliced
- 2 fresh red chilies, halved lengthways, seeds removed (optional for less spice), and sliced
- 1 sheet (approximately 18cm2) nori (toasted seaweed), torn

- 1 teaspoon ground turmeric
- 1 teaspoon ground coriander
- ½ teaspoon ground cumin
- 1 teaspoon sweet ground paprika

Soup:

- 200g sugar snap peas, trimmed and halved diagonally
- 200g green beans, trimmed and halved horizontally
- 2 bulbs pak choi, trimmed and roughly chopped
- 1 tablespoon vegetable oil
- 300g firm tofu, cut into 1cm cubes
- 400ml coconut milk
- 400ml low-salt vegetable stock
- 1 tablespoon palm sugar (or caster sugar)
- 200g dried wide flat brown rice noodles
- 100g fresh bean sprouts (optional)
- 100g cucumber, sliced into thin strips (optional)
- 3 spring onions, trimmed and thinly sliced diagonally (optional)
- Handful of mint and coriander leaves (optional)
- 1 lime, cut into 4 wedges (optional)

Preparation:

1. Laksa Paste: Blitz all laksa paste ingredients in a food processor until a smooth paste forms. Scrape down the sides as needed.

This may yield more paste than required; freeze half for later use.

2. Heat a large frying pan, add laksa paste, and fry over medium heat for 10 minutes until fragrant.
3. While the paste is frying, blanch sugar snap peas, green beans, and pak choi in boiling water. Drain and set aside.
4. Add oil and tofu to the pan with the fragrant paste. Stir to coat tofu, fry for about 3 minutes until lightly browned. Add coconut milk, sugar, reserved lemongrass parts, and vegetable stock. Bring to a gentle boil and simmer for 3 minutes.
5. Cook noodles according to package instructions, and drain thoroughly. Remove reserved lemongrass from the pan after 3 minutes of simmering.
6. Add cooked vegetables to the soup, bring to a simmer, and cook for 1 minute. Divide noodles between 4 bowls, ladle soup over noodles, and top with optional bean sprouts, cucumber, spring onions, and herbs. Serve immediately with lime wedges.

Tips:

- This vegetarian laksa is a twist on the classic Singapore dish, featuring herbs, spices, coconut milk, and low-potassium vegetables.

- Adjustments may be needed based on individual kidney diet guidelines; consult your dietitian or doctor for personalized advice.

Vegan Beetroot and Carrot Fritters

Meal Types: Main Meal | Prep Time: 20 mins | Cooking Time: 20 mins | Serving Size: 4 |

Ingredients:

- 200g chickpea flour (gram flour)
- 200g raw beetroot, peeled and grated
- 200g carrots, peeled and grated
- 8 spring onions, chopped
- 1 tablespoon olive oil

To Serve:

- 80g rocket leaves
- ½ cucumber, sliced
- 80 ml soya yogurt
- Small handful parsley, chopped
- 4 crusty rolls

Method:

1. Preheat the oven to 180°C/160°C fan/gas mark 4. Put the chickpea (gram) flour into a bowl and add the grated beetroot, carrots, and chopped onions. Mix to fully combine.
2. Add water gradually, only enough to bind the ingredients together. Heat the oil in a

frying pan over medium heat, divide the batter into eight fritters, and add to the frying pan. Cook for 3 minutes until the bottom has started to crisp, then flip the fritters and cook on the other side for another 3 minutes.

3. Transfer the fritters to a baking sheet and cook in the oven for 10 minutes. While the fritters are cooking, mix the chopped parsley into the yogurt.
4. Remove the fritters from the oven and serve two fritters per portion with the rocket and cucumber salad, yogurt, and a crusty roll.

Tips: *Adjustments may be needed based on individual kidney diet guidelines; consult your dietitian or doctor for personalized advice.*

Vegan Coronation Cauliflower

Meal Types: Main Meal | Prep Time: 20 mins | Cooking Time: 40 mins | Serving Size: 4 |

Ingredients:

- 1 large cauliflower (up to 850g), separated into florets
- 2 tablespoons medium curry powder
- 1 tablespoon olive oil
- 250g soya yogurt

- 20g sultanas
- 20g coriander, chopped
- 100g rocket or other salad leaves

Flatbreads:

- 200g plain flour
- 20g parsley, chopped
- 100ml water
- 2 tablespoons olive oil
- Up to 1 tablespoon of oil to cook the flatbreads

Preparation:

1. Add the cauliflower to a saucepan, fill with water, bring to a boil, and allow to boil for 3 minutes to keep it fairly firm. Drain and let it cool slightly. Preheat the oven to 200°C / 180°C fan/gas mark 6. Put the cauliflower into a roasting tin, and toss with two teaspoons of curry powder and one tablespoon of olive oil. Roast for 20 minutes.
2. While the cauliflower is cooking, mix the yogurt with the remaining curry powder, sultanas, and half of the chopped coriander.
3. Remove the cauliflower from the oven and let it cool slightly. Once cooled, mix it into the yogurt mixture.
4. Put the flour and parsley into a bowl, and mix in the water. Add in the oil, mix to form a dough, and then knead for five minutes.

5. Divide the dough into four pieces and roll it out on a floured surface. Heat a small amount of oil in a large frying pan and cook each flatbread for about two minutes on each side. Keep the dish warm by wrapping it in a clean tea towel until it's ready to be served.
6. Serve the cauliflower, sprinkled with the remaining coriander, with a flatbread and some salad leaves like a rocket.

Tip: *Place any remaining portions in an airtight container and store them in the refrigerator for up to 2 days. Reheat gently before serving if desired.*

Vibrant Vegetable and Tofu Stir-Fry

Meal Type : Main Dishes

Ingredients:

- 1 cup long-grain rice
- 2 ½ tbsp hoisin sauce
- 2 tbsp fresh lime juice
- 1 package (454g) medium-firm tofu, prepared with calcium sulfate, cut into ½-inch cubes
- 1 tbsp canola oil
- 1 carrot, cut into thin strips
- 1 bell pepper, thinly sliced

- 1 tbsp grated fresh ginger
- 2 cups bean sprouts
- 4 scallions, thinly sliced
- 2 tbsp roasted peanuts, roughly chopped
- ¼ cup fresh cilantro

Directions:

1. Cook the rice.
2. Whisk together hoisin sauce with lime juice.
3. Heat some oil in a big frying pan on a medium-high flame. Add carrot, bell pepper, and ginger; cook, stirring, for 2 minutes. Add tofu and bean sprouts. Cook, stirring, until the vegetables are slightly tender, 3 to 4 minutes. Ensure bean sprouts are fully cooked for food safety.
4. Toss the vegetables with the hoisin sauce mixture and serve over rice.
5. Sprinkle with scallions, peanuts, and cilantro, if desired.

Sesame Asparagus Recipe

Ingredients:

- 16 asparagus spears
- 1 tbsp lemon juice
- 2 tbsp sesame oil
- 1 tsp sesame seeds

Directions:

1. Mix asparagus with sesame oil, lemon juice, and sesame seeds.
2. Wrap in foil and bake at 375°F for 12-15 minutes until tender.

Eggplant and Tofu Stir-Fry Recipe

Ingredients:

- 1 cup long-grain white rice
- 2 tbsp hoisin sauce
- 3 tbsp rice vinegar
- 1 tsp cornstarch
- 4 tbsp canola oil
- 1 package (454g) medium firm Tofu, prepared with calcium sulfate, cut into 1-inch squares
- 1 small eggplant
- 4 scallions, sliced
- 2 cloves of garlic, chopped
- 1 red serrano or jalapeno pepper
- ¼ cup fresh basil leaves, torn

Directions:

1. Cook rice according to package instructions.
2. Warm 1 tablespoon of oil in a nonstick pan. Add tofu; turn occasionally until brown, approximately 10 minutes. Transfer to a plate.
3. Add remaining oil. Add vegetables, and cook until tender. Add sauce and then tofu.

Toss until the sauce is thickened. Serve with rice and topped with basil.

Roasted Cauliflower with Rosemary Recipe

Ingredients:

- 1 medium-head cauliflower
- 1-½ tablespoons olive oil
- 1 tablespoon fresh rosemary, finely chopped
- ¼ teaspoon salt
- Fresh ground black pepper

Directions:

1. Preheat the oven to 450oF.
2. Cut florets from the cauliflower head and break or cut them into bite-size pieces.
3. In a large bowl, toss cauliflower with the remaining ingredients.
4. Spread seasoned cauliflower on an ungreased baking sheet.
5. Roast for 15 minutes; remove from the oven and stir.
6. Continue cooking for 10 minutes or until cauliflower is fork-tender and lightly browned.

Easy Fresh Lemonade

Ingredients:

- 2 large lemons
- 8 cups of water

Directions:

1. Squeeze 2 large lemons (½ cup lemon juice) into 8 cups of water. Opt for a conventional manual juicer to extract the liquid or purchase pre-squeezed lemon juice as an alternative.
2. Serve with ice cubes and a hint of mint for flavor. Drink throughout the day.
3. You can add sugar or a sugar substitute if desired but try to limit your sugar to reduce your risk of stones.

Pineapple and Nectarine Kebabs

Meal Types: Dessert | Prep Time: 10 mins | Cooking Time: 5 mins | Serving Size: 4 |

Ingredients:

- 2 cans of pineapple chunks, each weighing 425 grams, with the juice discarded
- 2 large nectarines
- 1 tablespoon caster sugar
- 250g soya vanilla ice cream
- Handful of basil leaves

Preparation:

1. Soak eight wooden skewers in cold water.
2. Remove and discard the juice from the pineapple chunks by draining them.
3. Cut the nectarines into wedges.
4. Thread the fruit onto the skewers, alternating pineapple and nectarine. Sprinkle it with sugar.
5. Cook the skewers on a griddle pan over medium-high heat or under a grill for about five minutes.
6. While the kebabs are cooking, mix the remaining pineapple and a few chopped basil leaves for a quick salsa.
7. Arrange the fruit kebabs on top of the pineapple salsa, and serve with soy vanilla ice cream and a few basil leaves.

Tips:

- Enjoy immediately. For any leftovers, store them in the refrigerator for up to 1 day. The texture of the fruit may change upon refrigeration, so it's best when freshly prepared.
- Adjustments may be needed based on individual kidney diet guidelines; consult your dietitian or doctor for personalized advice.

Nut and Aubergine Roast

Meal Types: Main meal | Prep Time: 30 mins | Cooking Time: 50 mins | Serving Size: 4 |

Ingredients:

Nut Roast (8 portions, 4 can be frozen):

- 2 tablespoons olive oil
- 1 onion, finely chopped
- 1 clove garlic, crushed
- 50g button mushrooms, finely chopped
- 50g aubergine, finely chopped
- 2 carrots, grated
- 40g breadcrumbs
- 100g 'Rice & Quinoa' pouch
- Black pepper
- 250g mixed nuts, chopped
- 30g parsley, finely chopped
- Half a very low-salt vegetable stock cube

Potatoes and Vegetables:

- 500g (4) medium potatoes, peeled
- 2 tablespoons olive oil
- 250g swede, peeled
- 40g vegan dairy-free spread
- 250g spring greens, shredded, or 250g carrots, peeled and chopped
- Cracked black pepper

Gravy:

Use a low-salt vegan gravy made to packet instructions

Preparation:

Nut Roast:

1. Heat oven to 175°C/155°C fan/gas mark 3 and oil a silicone 907g (2lb) loaf tin or line a metal loaf tin with parchment paper.
2. In a frying pan, heat the remaining oil and sauté the onion and garlic until soft.
3. Add the mushrooms, aubergine, and carrot to the frying pan and sauté until soft.
4. In a bowl, mix the breadcrumbs, rice, and quinoa with black pepper and nuts.
5. Add the sautéed vegetables, chopped parsley, and vegetable stock (made with 50ml of boiling water), then mix until well combined.
6. Pour the mixture into the loaf tin and press down to ensure it is evenly spread and firm. Bake for 40 minutes.

Potatoes and Vegetables:

1. Chop the potatoes into 4 and put into a pan with cold water. Boil until soft. Drain and shake the potatoes in the colander to rough the edges up a little. Cover with a tea towel.
2. Put a roasting tin into the oven with olive oil and heat for five minutes, then remove and add the parboiled potatoes, turning them to coat them in oil. Return to the oven for 45 minutes.

3. Cut the swede into chunks and boil until soft. Drain the swede and put it back into the pan. Add vegan spread and black pepper to taste and mash.
4. About 10 minutes before serving, add the spring greens or carrots to a saucepan of water and boil until cooked, then drain.
5. Once cooked, remove the nut roast from the oven and leave to cool in the tin for 10 minutes.
6. Make the gravy as per the packet instructions.

Assembly:

Serve the nut roast with prepared vegetables, and potatoes, and pour over your desired amount of gravy.

Tips:

- This recipe makes eight portions, so four can be served fresh while saving the rest for another day.
- Enjoy immediately. For any leftovers, store them in the refrigerator for up to 1 day. The texture of the nut roast may change upon refrigeration, so it's best when freshly prepared.

Note: Adjustments may be needed based on individual kidney diet guidelines; consult your dietitian or doctor for personalized advice.

Stuffed Scary Pepper Faces

Ingredients:

- 120g red lentils, dried
- 1 tablespoon vegetable oil
- 1 onion, finely chopped
- 2 garlic cloves, crushed or finely chopped
- 1cm fresh ginger, grated or finely chopped
- 1 teaspoon tomato purée
- 1 teaspoon ground cumin
- 1 teaspoon garam masala
- 200g basmati rice
- 1 low-salt vegetable stock cube
- 850ml water, boiling
- 20g mint leaves, fresh
- 8 peppers (yellow red, and orange work well)

Instructions:

1. Preheat the oven to 200°C (392°F) or 180°C (356°F) for fan-assisted ovens, or gas mark 6. Wash the dried lentils and set aside to drain.
2. Warm the oil in a sizable saucepan with a lid. Add the onion, garlic, and ginger. Gently cook on low heat for 5 minutes until softened.
3. Stir in the tomato purée and spices. Cook for a further minute.

4. Add the rice. Stir well. Make up the vegetable stock and pour over the rice. Bring to a boil, then add the lentils.
5. Cover with the lid and leave to cook over low heat for 15 minutes until the lentils and rice are cooked. Coarsely chop the mint and mix it in.

Assembling Scary Pepper Faces:

1. Slice the top off each pepper, cut out the stalk, and scoop out the seeds.
2. Cut a spooky face into the side of the peppers. Carefully cut a flat surface onto the bottom of the peppers so they stand upright, ensuring you don't create a hole in the bottom.
3. Place the peppers in a lightly greased baking dish.
4. Fill each pepper with the rice mixture and place the pepper lid on top.
5. Cook for 25-30 minutes or until the peppers have softened and begun to color.
6. Serve two per person for a main meal or one each for a party snack.

North African One-Pot Casserole

Ingredients:

- 2 tablespoons of olive oil
- 1 onion

- 2 garlic cloves
- 1 teaspoon smoked paprika
- ½ teaspoon ground cumin
- ½ teaspoon ground cinnamon
- ½ teaspoon ground ginger
- 1 red pepper
- 1 yellow pepper
- 1 celery stick
- 2 courgettes
- Sprig of fresh thyme
- 1 bay leaf
- 150g butternut squash
- 125g drained, tinned cooked lentils
- 125g drained, tinned cooked chickpeas
- 400g tinned tomatoes
- 250ml vegetable stock
- Handful of fresh parsley
- Pinch saffron strands (optional)

To serve:

- Flatbread or crusty roll (approx. 125g each)

Instructions:

1. Prepare all the vegetables, dice them into similar-sized pieces, and set aside. Warm the oil in a large, heavy-based pan. Add the onion and garlic and cook over a gentle heat until onions and garlic soften.
2. Add the spices (including the saffron if you are using it) and cook for a further few minutes to release the flavors of the spice.

This step is crucial in the process. If the spices are not allowed to completely cook through, you will end up with a sharp and bitter taste to the finished dish.

3. Add the celery and peppers and cook for a further 5 minutes. Add the butternut squash, fresh thyme, and bay leaf. Add tinned tomatoes and the stock. Simmer for 20-25 minutes until the squash is just about cooked through. After 15 minutes, add the courgettes.
4. Stir in the lentils and chickpeas and bring back to a simmer for 5-10 minutes. Add the chopped parsley and coriander and serve. This dish is delicious with warmed flatbread, pitta, or crusty roll.

Rice and Bean Burrito with Side Salad

Ingredients:

Burrito:

- 250g brown rice
- 1 lime
- 15g fresh coriander
- 1 small onion
- 3 garlic cloves
- 2 tablespoons vegetable oil
- 400g kidney beans
- 200g sweetcorn

- 1 teaspoon chili powder
- ½ teaspoon cumin
- 1 tablespoon hot sauce (to taste)
- 4 large tortilla wraps

Side Salad:

- ½ iceberg lettuce
- 1 red, yellow, or orange pepper
- 3 spring onions
- ¼ cucumber

Instructions:

1. Rinse rice under cold running water, then add to a saucepan and pour over 500ml of water. Bring the mixture to a boil, then decrease the heat to a gentle simmer. Cook for 30 minutes, then drain and rinse with boiling water. Add the juice of the lime and chop the coriander into the rice, stirring gently.
2. Peel and finely chop the onion and crush the garlic. In a pan, add the vegetable oil and gently fry the onion until soft, then add the garlic and cook for another 1-2 minutes.
3. Add the beans, chili powder, cumin, and hot sauce (if using) to the onion and garlic. Stir to combine. Allow the beans to cook until heated through and soft, about 5-10 minutes. Keep them whole or gently press on them with the back of a fork for a mushy texture.

4. After the beans are cooked, drain them and then add the sweetcorn. Cook until the sweetcorn is warmed through. Heat the tortillas by microwaving them under a damp paper towel for 15-30 seconds or on a griddle over low heat.
5. For the side salad, wash and shred the lettuce. Remove the seeds from the pepper, slice it, trim and slice the spring onions, and slice the cucumber. Place all the prepared salad ingredients into a large bowl and mix well, then divide into 4 portions.
6. Add the rice filling to the bottom half of the tortilla. Fold the bottom of the tortilla up and over the filling, pulling the filling back tight toward the bottom. Make two folds on either side, keeping the filling snug inside. Roll it up! Eat whole or cut in half and serve with the side salad.

"Cooking is an art, and every ingredient is a brushstroke on the canvas of your health.Nourish your body, nurture your soul. Every bite you take is an opportunity to heal and thrive."

- Nancy K. Doctor

CONCLUSION

"Vegan Diet Cookbook For Kidney Disease" is more than just a collection of recipes – it's a guide to transforming your health and embracing a new way of life. Through the pages of this book, you've discovered the incredible healing power of plant-based foods and learned how simple dietary changes can have a profound impact on your well-being.

As a nephrologist and author, I've seen firsthand the struggles that come with kidney disease, but I've also witnessed the remarkable resilience of the human spirit. With dedication, determination, and a little help from the kitchen, you can take control of your health and thrive despite any obstacles you may face.

Remember, healing is not just about treating the symptoms – it's about nourishing your body, mind, and soul. So, as you embark on your journey to better health, I encourage you to approach each recipe with an open heart and a sense of adventure. Embrace the flavors, savor the moments, and most importantly, listen to your body. Every meal is an opportunity to heal, thrive, and embrace life to the fullest. Here's to your health, happiness, and a future filled with delicious, kidney-friendly meals.

Thank you for allowing me to be a part of your journey. May this cookbook serve as a beacon of hope and inspiration as you take the next steps toward a happier, healthier life.

Nancy K. Doctor

BONUS

42 DAYS MEAL PLAN

Week 1:

Day 1:

- Breakfast: Peach Raspberry Smoothie
- Lunch: Vegan Bean Bourguignon
- Dinner: Light and Cheesy Summer Zucchini Lasagna
- Snack: Savory Snack Mix

Day 2:

- Breakfast: Roasted Red Pepper & Chickpea Hummus on Vegan Gluten-Free White Bread
- Lunch: Hearty Vegetable Stew
- Dinner: Plant-Powered Bean Stew with Fragrant Basmati Rice Grains & Pasta
- Snack: Fresh Zippy Strawberry Salad

Day 3:

- Breakfast: Vegan Tofu and Veggie Frittata
- Lunch: Zucchini-Carrot Soup
- Dinner: Butternut Bliss Pasta Bake
- Snack: Easy Pear and Arugula Salad

Day 4:

- Breakfast: Tomato-Lentil Delight
- Lunch: Savory Roasted Cabbage Wedges

- Dinner: Spicy Black Bean Tacos with Roasted Vegetables
- Snack: Icy Smoothie

Day 5:

- Breakfast: Lemon Hummus with Toasted Vegan Gluten-Free White Bread
- Lunch: Asian Eggplant Dip with Mediterranean Bean and Couscous Salad
- Dinner: Vegan Gluten-Free White Bread with Plant-Based Indian-Inspired Stuffed Peppers
- Snack: Corn and Cilantro Salsa

Day 6:

- Breakfast: Fragrant Basmati Rice Grains & Pasta
- Lunch: Sweet & Crunchy Coleslaw with Renal Mushroom Pockets
- Dinner: Nut and Aubergine Roast with Sesame Asparagus
- Snack: Pineapple and Nectarine Kebabs

Day 7:

- Breakfast: Fruity Oat Crisp Delight
- Lunch: North African One-Pot Casserole
- Dinner: Rice and Bean Burrito with Side Salad
- Snack: Plant-Based Vegetable Laksa with Sugar Snap Peas and Pak Choi

Week 2:

Day 8:

- Breakfast: Vegan Coronation Cauliflower
- Lunch: Vibrant Vegetable and Tofu Stir-Fry
- Dinner: Eggplant & Chickpea Bites with Sesame Asparagus Recipe
- Snack: Easy Fresh Lemonade

Day 9:

- Breakfast: Red Velvet Loaf Cake
- Lunch: Mediterranean Green Beans
- Dinner: Stuffed Scary Pepper Faces
- Snack: Sweet Cauliflower with Fresh Dill

Day 10:

- Breakfast: Vegan Herbs Pasta
- Lunch: Garlicky Swiss Chard Bliss with Sweet & Crunchy Coleslaw
- Dinner: Eggplant and Tofu Stir-Fry Recipe
- Snack: Roasted Red Pepper Coulis

Day 11:

- Breakfast: Spicy Hot Cereal
- Lunch: Savory Roasted Red Pepper Delight with Aromatic Herbed Rice
- Dinner: Easy and Light-Tasting Coleslaw with Lemony Orzo Salad
- Snack: Corn and Cilantro Salsa

Day 12:

- Breakfast: The Green Beans Garlic Salad Veggies

- Lunch: Fragrant Basmati Rice Grains & Pasta with Zesty Pina Colada Smoothie
- Dinner: Tomato-Lentil Delight
- Snack: Icy Smoothie

Day 13:

- Breakfast: Tasty Double Boiled Mashed Potatoes
- Lunch: Curried Eggplant Mix with Cucumber Salad
- Dinner: Vegan Beetroot and Carrot Fritters with Aromatic Basmati Rice and Seasonal Fresh Herbs
- Snack: Asian Eggplant Dip

Day 14:

- Breakfast: Sweet & Crunchy Coleslaw
- Lunch: Mediterranean Bean and Couscous Salad
- Dinner: Light and Cheesy Summer Zucchini Lasagna
- Snack: Fresh Zippy Strawberry Salad

Week 3:

Day 15:

- Breakfast: Nut and Aubergine Roast
- Lunch: Vegan Gluten-Free White Bread with Roasted Cauliflower with Rosemary Recipe
- Dinner: Vegan Bean Bourguignon
- Snack: Pineapple and Nectarine Kebabs

Day 16:

- Breakfast: Rice and Bean Burrito with Side Salad
- Lunch: North African One-Pot Casserole
- Dinner: Plant-Powered Bean Stew
- Snack: Lemon Hummus

Day 17:

- Breakfast: Aromatic Basmati Rice and Seasonal Fresh Herbs
- Lunch: Hearty Vegetable Stew
- Dinner: Vegan Instant Hearty and Bean Chili
- Snack: Fruity Oat Crisp Delight

Day 18:

- Breakfast: Savory Snack Mix
- Lunch: Easy Tarragon Dressing with Salad
- Dinner: Hearty Shiitake Elixir with Roasted Cabbage Wedges
- Snack: Savory Roasted Cabbage Wedges

Day 19:

- Breakfast: Aromatic Herbed Rice
- Lunch: Zucchini-Carrot Soup with Asian Apple Slaw
- Dinner: Plant-Based Vegetable Laksa with Sugar Snap Peas and Pak Choi
- Snack: Peach Raspberry Smoothie

Day 20:

- Breakfast: Double Cranberry Pear Crisp
- Lunch: Mediterranean Bean and Couscous Salad

- Dinner: Butternut Bliss Pasta Bake
- Snack: Zucchini Corn Sauté Sandwiches & Wraps

Day 21:

- Breakfast: Fresh Zippy Strawberry Salad
- Lunch: Curried Eggplant Mix with Cucumber Salad
- Dinner: Vegan Gluten-Free White Bread
- Snack: Easy Pear and Arugula Salad

Week 4:

Day 22:

- Breakfast: Roasted Red Pepper Coulis
- Lunch: Fragrant Basmati Rice Grains & Pasta
- Dinner: Vegan Coronation Cauliflower
- Snack: Spicy Hot Cereal

Day 23:

- Breakfast: Sesame Asparagus Recipe
- Lunch: Rooh Afza Lemonade with Vegan Beetroot and Carrot Fritters
- Dinner: Eggplant & Chickpea Bites
- Snack: Corn and Cilantro Salsa

Day 24:

- Breakfast: Lemon Hummus
- Lunch: Stuffed Scary Pepper Faces
- Dinner: Light and Cheesy Summer Zucchini Lasagna
- Snack: Renal Mushroom Pockets

Day 25:

- Breakfast: Garlicky Swiss Chard Bliss
- Lunch: Savory Tofu Fingers Delight with Sweet & Crunchy Coleslaw
- Dinner: Tomato-Lentil Delight
- Snack: Icy Smoothie

Day 26:

- Breakfast: Zesty Pina Colada Smoothie
- Lunch: Vegan Herbs Pasta with Easy Fresh Lemonade
- Dinner: Mediterranean Green Beans
- Snack: Roasted Red Pepper & Chickpea Hummus with Carrot Sticks

Day 27:

- Breakfast: Savory Roasted Red Pepper Delight
- Lunch: Eggplant and Tofu Stir-Fry Recipe
- Dinner: Spicy Black Bean Tacos with Roasted Vegetables
- Snack: Pineapple and Nectarine Kebabs

Day 28:

- Breakfast: Easy Tarragon Dressing with Salad
- Lunch: Sweet Cauliflower with Fresh Dill
- Dinner: Vegan Gluten-Free White Bread with Nut and Aubergine Roast
- Snack: Fresh Zippy Strawberry Salad

Week 5:

Day 29:

- Breakfast: Aromatic Basmati Rice and Seasonal Fresh Herbs
- Lunch: Hearty Vegetable Stew
- Dinner: Asian Eggplant Dip with Rice and Bean Burrito
- Snack: Peach Raspberry Smoothie

Day 30:

- Breakfast: Warm Mushroom Salad with Watercress
- Lunch: Mediterranean Bean and Couscous Salad
- Dinner: Plant-Based Vegetable Laksa with Sugar Snap Peas and Pak Choi
- Snack: Corn and Cilantro Salsa

Day 31:

- Breakfast: Fragrant Basmati Rice Grains & Pasta
- Lunch: Spicy Hot Cereal
- Dinner: North African One-Pot Casserole
- Snack: Easy Pear and Arugula Salad

Day 32:

- Breakfast: Vegan Gluten-Free White Bread
- Lunch: Hearty Shiitake Elixir
- Dinner: Vibrant Vegetable and Tofu Stir-Fry
- Snack: Sesame Asparagus Recipe

Day 33:

- Breakfast: Easy and Light-Tasting Coleslaw

- Lunch: Vegan Tofu and Veggie Frittata
- Dinner: Eggplant & Chickpea Bites
- Snack: Spicy Red Velvet Loaf Cake

Day 34:

- Breakfast: Savory Roasted Cabbage Wedges
- Lunch: Plant-Powered Bean Stew
- Dinner: Butternut Bliss Pasta Bake
- Snack: Nut and Aubergine Roast

Day 35:

- Breakfast: Lemon Hummus
- Lunch: Light and Cheesy Summer Zucchini Lasagna
- Dinner: Tomato-Lentil Delight
- Snack: Easy Fresh Lemonade

Week 6:

Day 36:

- Breakfast: Fragrant Basmati Rice Grains & Pasta
- Lunch: Vegan Beetroot and Carrot Fritters
- Dinner: Savory Tofu Fingers Delight
- Snack: Icy Smoothie

Day 37:

- Breakfast: Nut and Aubergine Roast
- Lunch: Roasted Red Pepper & Chickpea Hummus with Renal Mushroom Pockets
- Dinner: Stuffed Scary Pepper Faces
- Snack: Pineapple and Nectarine Kebabs

Day 38:

- Breakfast: Sesame Asparagus Recipe
- Lunch: Mediterranean Green Beans
- Dinner: Eggplant and Tofu Stir-Fry Recipe
- Snack: Lemon Hummus

Day 39:

- Breakfast: Easy Tarragon Dressing with Salad
- Lunch: Vegan Coronation Cauliflower
- Dinner: Sweet Cauliflower with Fresh Dill
- Snack: Corn and Cilantro Salsa

Day 40:

- Breakfast: Zesty Pina Colada Smoothie
- Lunch: Red Velvet Loaf Cake
- Dinner: Roasted Cauliflower with Rosemary Recipe
- Snack: Spicy Hot Cereal

Day 41:

- Breakfast: Savory Roasted Red Pepper Delight
- Lunch: Light and Cheesy Summer Zucchini Lasagna
- Dinner: Plant-Based Indian-Inspired Stuffed Peppers
- Snack: Easy Fresh Lemonade

Day 42:

- Breakfast: Fragrant Basmati Rice Grains & Pasta
- Lunch: Roasted Red Pepper Coulis

- Dinner: Rice and Bean Burrito with Side Salad
- Snack: Peach Raspberry Smoothie

8 WEEKS FOOD JOURNAL

VEGAN MEAL JOURNAL

WEEK: ______________ DATE: ______________

Breakfast
Lunch
Dinner
Snacks
Rating your day ○○○○○

Breakfast
Lunch
Dinner
Snacks
Rating your day ○○○○○

Breakfast
Lunch
Dinner
Snacks
Rating your day ○○○○○

Breakfast
Lunch
Dinner
Snacks
Rating your day ○○○○○

Breakfast
Lunch
Dinner
Snacks
Rating your day ○○○○○

Breakfast
Lunch
Dinner
Snacks
Rating your day ○○○○○

Breakfast
Lunch
Dinner
Snacks
Rating your day ○○○○○

OBSERVATIONS:

VEGAN MEAL JOURNAL

WEEK:

DATE:

Breakfast
Lunch
Dinner
Snacks
Rating your day ○○○○○

Breakfast
Lunch
Dinner
Snacks
Rating your day ○○○○○

Breakfast
Lunch
Dinner
Snacks
Rating your day ○○○○○

Breakfast
Lunch
Dinner
Snacks
Rating your day ○○○○○

Breakfast
Lunch
Dinner
Snacks
Rating your day ○○○○○

Breakfast
Lunch
Dinner
Snacks
Rating your day ○○○○○

Breakfast
Lunch
Dinner
Snacks
Rating your day ○○○○○

OBSERVATIONS:

VEGAN MEAL JOURNAL

WEEK: ____________ DATE: ____________

Breakfast
Lunch
Dinner
Snacks
Rating your day ○○○○○

Breakfast
Lunch
Dinner
Snacks
Rating your day ○○○○○

Breakfast
Lunch
Dinner
Snacks
Rating your day ○○○○○

Breakfast
Lunch
Dinner
Snacks
Rating your day ○○○○○

Breakfast
Lunch
Dinner
Snacks
Rating your day ○○○○○

Breakfast
Lunch
Dinner
Snacks
Rating your day ○○○○○

Breakfast
Lunch
Dinner
Snacks
Rating your day ○○○○○

OBSERVATIONS:

VEGAN MEAL JOURNAL

WEEK: ____________ DATE: ____________

Breakfast
Lunch
Dinner
Snacks
Rating your day ○○○○○

Breakfast
Lunch
Dinner
Snacks
Rating your day ○○○○○

Breakfast
Lunch
Dinner
Snacks
Rating your day ○○○○○

Breakfast
Lunch
Dinner
Snacks
Rating your day ○○○○○

Breakfast
Lunch
Dinner
Snacks
Rating your day ○○○○○

Breakfast
Lunch
Dinner
Snacks
Rating your day ○○○○○

Breakfast
Lunch
Dinner
Snacks
Rating your day ○○○○○

OBSERVATIONS:

VEGAN MEAL JOURNAL

WEEK: ____________ DATE: ____________

Breakfast
Lunch
Dinner
Snacks
Rating your day ○○○○○

Breakfast
Lunch
Dinner
Snacks
Rating your day ○○○○○

Breakfast
Lunch
Dinner
Snacks
Rating your day ○○○○○

Breakfast
Lunch
Dinner
Snacks
Rating your day ○○○○○

Breakfast
Lunch
Dinner
Snacks
Rating your day ○○○○○

Breakfast
Lunch
Dinner
Snacks
Rating your day ○○○○○

Breakfast
Lunch
Dinner
Snacks
Rating your day ○○○○○

OBSERVATIONS:

VEGAN MEAL JOURNAL

WEEK: ____________________ DATE: ____________________

Breakfast
Lunch
Dinner
Snacks
Rating your day ○○○○○

Breakfast
Lunch
Dinner
Snacks
Rating your day ○○○○○

Breakfast
Lunch
Dinner
Snacks
Rating your day ○○○○○

Breakfast
Lunch
Dinner
Snacks
Rating your day ○○○○○

Breakfast
Lunch
Dinner
Snacks
Rating your day ○○○○○

Breakfast
Lunch
Dinner
Snacks
Rating your day ○○○○○

Breakfast
Lunch
Dinner
Snacks
Rating your day ○○○○○

OBSERVATIONS:

VEGAN MEAL JOURNAL

WEEK: DATE:

Breakfast
Lunch
Dinner
Snacks
Rating your day ○○○○○

Breakfast
Lunch
Dinner
Snacks
Rating your day ○○○○○

Breakfast
Lunch
Dinner
Snacks
Rating your day ○○○○○

Breakfast
Lunch
Dinner
Snacks
Rating your day ○○○○○

Breakfast
Lunch
Dinner
Snacks
Rating your day ○○○○○

Breakfast
Lunch
Dinner
Snacks
Rating your day ○○○○○

Breakfast
Lunch
Dinner
Snacks
Rating your day ○○○○○

OBSERVATIONS:

VEGAN MEAL JOURNAL

WEEK: ____________ DATE: ____________

Breakfast
Lunch
Dinner
Snacks
Rating your day ○○○○○

Breakfast
Lunch
Dinner
Snacks
Rating your day ○○○○○

Breakfast
Lunch
Dinner
Snacks
Rating your day ○○○○○

Breakfast
Lunch
Dinner
Snacks
Rating your day ○○○○○

Breakfast
Lunch
Dinner
Snacks
Rating your day ○○○○○

Breakfast
Lunch
Dinner
Snacks
Rating your day ○○○○○

Breakfast
Lunch
Dinner
Snacks
Rating your day ○○○○○

OBSERVATIONS:

Groceries List Planner

MY GROCERY LIST
PANTRY
FRUITS
VEGETABLES
GRAINS
RICE
2KG
SNACKS
NOTES

MY GROCERY LIST
PANTRY
FRUITS
VEGETABLES
GRAINS
RICE
2KG
SNACKS
NOTES

MY GROCERY LIST
PANTRY
FRUITS
VEGETABLES
GRAINS
RICE
2KG
SNACKS
NOTES

MY GROCERY LIST
PANTRY
FRUITS
VEGETABLES
GRAINS
RICE
2KG
SNACKS
NOTES

MY GROCERY LIST
PANTRY
FRUITS
VEGETABLES
GRAINS
RICE
2KG
SNACKS
NOTES

MY GROCERY LIST
PANTRY
FRUITS
VEGETABLES
GRAINS
RICE
SNACKS
NOTES

MY GROCERY LIST
PANTRY
FRUITS
VEGETABLES
GRAINS
RICE
2KG
SNACKS
NOTES

Free Ebook Download

Scan The QR Code below with Your Phone to download the Ebook version of this Cookbook 👇

ABOUT THE AUTHOR

Dr. Nancy K. Doctor, a passionate advocate for kidney health, has dedicated her career to empowering individuals affected by kidney disease. As a renowned nephrologist, certified dietician, and seasoned fitness coach, she brings a unique perspective to the field, merging medical knowledge with practical dietary and lifestyle solutions.

For over two decades, Dr. Nancy has guided countless patients through the complexities of kidney disease, helping them navigate dietary limitations and embrace healthier living. Her commitment extends beyond the clinic, as she actively inspires communities through lectures, workshops, and her bestselling books, "Renal Diet Cookbook For Seniors: Delicious and Easy to make Recipes that Support Kidney Health and are low in Sodium and Potassium."

Driven by a belief that delicious food and empowered choices can pave the way to renal well-being, Dr. Nancy is always on the lookout for innovative approaches. Witnessing the potential of air fryer technology to create exciting and flavorful kidney-friendly dishes spurred her latest project, "Vegan Diet Cookbook For Kidney Disease"

This book, though just one facet of Dr. Nancy's multifaceted contribution to kidney health, exemplifies her unwavering dedication to making delicious, nutritious food accessible for everyone on their renal journey. Whether through air fryer magic or other empowering resources, Dr. Nancy remains a beacon of hope, guiding individuals towards a healthier, happier life with kidney disease.

FOR OTHER BOOKS WRITTEN BY THE AUTHOR

Printed in Great Britain
by Amazon

63013365R00070